Cram101 Textbook Outlines to accompany:

Marketing Mistakes and Successes

Robert F. Hartley , 11th Edition

A Cram101 Inc. publication (c) 2010.

PRACTICE EXAMS.

Get all of the self-teaching practice exams for each chapter of this textbook at **www.Cram101.com** and ace the tests. Here is an example:

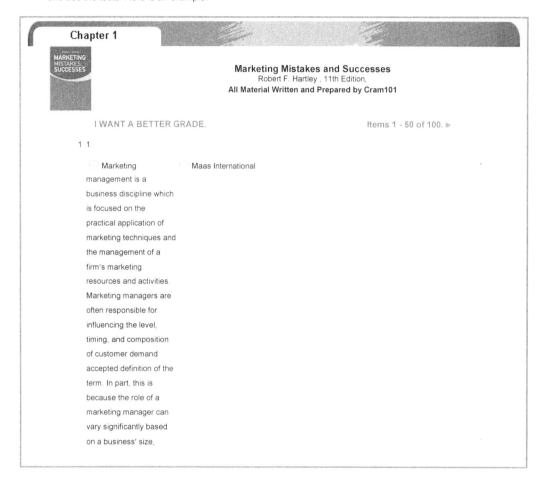

You get a 50% discount for the online exams. Go to **Cram101.com**, click Sign Up at the top of the screen, and enter DK73DW5562 in the promo code box on the registration screen. Access to Cram101.com is $4.95 per month, cancel at any time.

With Cram101.com online, you also have access to extensive reference material.

You will nail those essays and papers. Here is an example from a Cram101 Biology text:

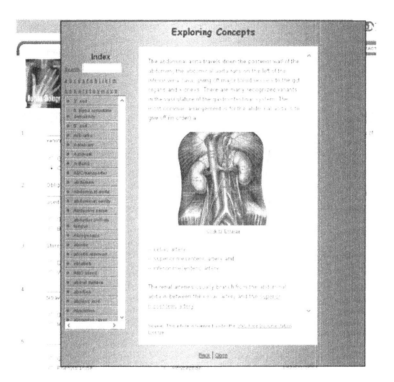

Visit **www.Cram101.com**, click Sign Up at the top of the screen, and enter DK73DW5562 in the promo code box on the registration screen. Access to www.Cram101.com is normally $9.95 per month, but because you have purchased this book, your access fee is only $4.95 per month, cancel at any time. Sign up and stop highlighting textbooks forever.

Learning System

Cram101 Textbook Outlines is a learning system. The notes in this book are the highlights of your textbook, you will never have to highlight a book again.

How to use this book. Take this book to class, it is your notebook for the lecture. The notes and highlights on the left hand side of the pages follow the outline and order of the textbook. All you have to do is follow along while your instructor presents the lecture. Circle the items emphasized in class and add other important information on the right side. With Cram101 Textbook Outlines you'll spend less time writing and more time listening. Learning becomes more efficient.

Cram101.com Online

Increase your studying efficiency by using Cram101.com's practice tests and online reference material. It is the perfect complement to Cram101 Textbook Outlines. Use self-teaching matching tests or simulate in-class testing with comprehensive multiple choice tests, or simply use Cram's true and false tests for quick review. Cram101.com even allows you to enter your in-class notes for an integrated studying format combining the textbook notes with your class notes.

Visit **www.Cram101.com**, click Sign Up at the top of the screen, and enter **DK73DW5562** in the promo code box on the registration screen. Access to www.Cram101.com is normally $9.95 per month, but because you have purchased this book, your access fee is only $4.95 per month. Sign up and stop highlighting textbooks forever.

Marketing Mistakes and Successes
Robert F. Hartley , 11th

CONTENTS

Marketing	marketing is a "social and managerial process by which individuals and groups obtain what they need and want through creating and exchanging products and values with others." It is an integrated process through which companies create value for customers and build strong customer relationships in order to capture value from customers in return. marketing is used to create the customer, to keep the customer and to satisfy the customer. With the customer as the focus of its activities, it can be concluded that marketing management is one of the major components of business management.
Marketing management	Marketing management is a business discipline which is focused on the practical application of marketing techniques and the management of a firm"s marketing resources and activities. Marketing managers are often responsible for influencing the level, timing, and composition of customer demand accepted definition of the term. In part, this is because the role of a marketing manager can vary significantly based on a business" size, corporate culture, and industry context.
Sergey Brin	Sergey Brin is founder of Google, Inc., the world"s largest internet company, based on its search engine and online advertising technology. He is ranked by Forbes as the 32nd richest person in the world. Brin emigrated to the United States at the age of six due to his family"s educational barriers in the Soviet Union.
Starbucks	Starbucks Corporation (NASDAQ: SBUX) is an international coffee and coffeehouse chain based in Seattle, Washington, USA. Starbucks is the largest coffeehouse company in the world, with 16,120 stores in 48 countries, including around 11,000 in the United States, nearly 1000 in Canada and more than 800 in Japan. Starbucks sells drip brewed coffee, espresso-based hot drinks, other hot and cold drinks, snacks, and items such as mugs and coffee beans.
Data migration	Data migration is the process of transferring data between storage types, formats, freeing up human resources from tedious tasks. It is required when organizations or individuals change computer systems or upgrade to new systems, or when systems merge (such as when the organizations that use them undergo a merger/takeover).
Reebok	Reebok International Limited, a subsidiary of German sportswear giant Adidas, is a producer of athletic footwear, apparel, and accessories. The name comes from the Afrikaans spelling of rhebok, a type of African antelope or gazelle. The company, founded in Bolton, England in 1895, was originally called J.W. Foster and Sons but was renamed Reebok in 1958.
Sears	Sears, Roebuck and Co., commonly known as Sears, is an American mid-range chain of international department stores, founded by Richard Warren Sears and Alvah Roebuck in the late 19th century. From its mail order beginnings, the company grew to become the largest retailer in the United States by the mid-20th century, and its catalogs became famous. Competition and changes in the demographics of its customer base challenged the company after World War II as its rural and inner city strongholds shrank and the suburban markets grew.
Southwest Airlines	Southwest Airlines Co. (NYSE: LUV) is an American low-cost airline with its largest focus city at Las Vegas" McCarran International Airport. Southwest is the largest airline in the United States by number of passengers carried domestically per year (as of December 31, 2007.)

Walt Disney	Walter Elias "Walt" Disney (December 5, 1901 - December 15, 1966) was an American film producer, director, screenwriter, voice actor, animator, entrepreneur, entertainer, international icon and philanthropist. Disney is famous for his influence in the field of entertainment during the twentieth century. As the co-founder (with his brother Roy O. Disney) of Walt Disney Productions, Disney became one of the best-known motion picture producers in the world.
Walt Disney Company	The Walt Disney Company is the largest media and entertainment corporation in the world. Founded on October 16, 1923, by brothers Walt and Roy Disney as an animation studio, it has become one of the biggest Hollywood studios, and owner and licensor of eleven theme parks and several television networks, including ABC and ESPN. Disney"s corporate headquarters and primary production facilities are located at The Walt Disney Studios in Burbank, California.
Rofecoxib	Rofecoxib is a nonsteroidal anti-inflammatory drug that has now been withdrawn over safety concerns. It was marketed by Merck ' Co. to treat osteoarthritis, acute pain conditions, and dysmenorrhoea.

IPO	An initial public stock offering (IPO) referred to simply as an "offering" or "flotation," is when a company issues common stock or shares to the public for the first time. They are often issued by smaller, younger companies seeking capital to expand, but can also be done by large privately-owned companies looking to become publicly traded.
	In an IPO the issuer may obtain the assistance of an underwriting firm, which helps it determine what type of security to issue (common or preferred), best offering price and time to bring it to market.
Sergey Brin	Sergey Brin is founder of Google, Inc., the world"s largest internet company, based on its search engine and online advertising technology. He is ranked by Forbes as the 32nd richest person in the world.
	Brin emigrated to the United States at the age of six due to his family"s educational barriers in the Soviet Union.
Celebrity branding	Celebrity branding is a type of branding, in which a celebrity uses his or her status in society to promote a product, service or charity. Celebrity branding can take several different forms, from a celebrity simply appearing in advertisements for a product, service or charity, to a celebrity attending PR events, creating his or her own line of products or services, and/or using his or her name as a brand. The most popular forms of celebrity brand lines are for clothing and fragrances.
Targeted advertising	Targeted advertising is a type of advertising whereby advertisements are placed so as to reach consumers based on various traits such as demographics, purchase history, or observed behavior.
	Two principal forms of targeted interactive advertising are behavioral targeting and contextual advertising.
Product	When a product reaches the maturity stage of the product life cycle a company may choose to operate strategies to extend the life of the product. If the product is predicted to continue to be successful or an upgrade is soon to be released the company can use various methods to keep sales, else the product will be left as is to continue to the decline stage.
	Examples of extension strategies are:
	· Discounted price · Increased advertising · Accessing another market abroad Another strategy is added value. This is a widely used extension strategy.
Yahoo	Yahoo! Inc. (NASDAQ: YHOO) is an American public corporation headquartered in Sunnyvale, California, (in Silicon Valley), that provides Internet services worldwide. The company is perhaps best known for its web portal, search engine, Yahoo! Directory, Yahoo! Mail, news, and social media websites and services.
Lee	Lee is a brand of denim jeans, first produced in 1889 in Salina, Kansas. The company is owned by VF Corporation, the largest apparel company in the world. Its headquarters are currently in Merriam near Kansas City, Kansas.
Cult	cult pejoratively refers to a religious group whose beliefs or practices could be considered strange or sinister. The term was originally used to denote a system of ritual practices. The narrower, derogatory sense of the word is a product of the 20th century, especially since the 1980s, and is a result of the anti-cult movement, which uses the term in reference to groups seen as authoritarian, exploitative and possibly dangerous.

Chapter 3. Starbucks: A Paragon of Growth and Employee Benefits Finds Storms

Starbucks	Starbucks Corporation (NASDAQ: SBUX) is an international coffee and coffeehouse chain based in Seattle, Washington, USA. Starbucks is the largest coffeehouse company in the world, with 16,120 stores in 48 countries, including around 11,000 in the United States, nearly 1000 in Canada and more than 800 in Japan. Starbucks sells drip brewed coffee, espresso-based hot drinks, other hot and cold drinks, snacks, and items such as mugs and coffee beans.
Competition	Co-operative competition is based upon promoting mutual survival - "everyone wins". Adam Smith"s "invisible hand" is a process where individuals compete to improve their level of happiness but compete in a cooperative manner through peaceful exchange and without violating other people. Cooperative competition focuses individuals/groups/organisms against the environment.
Boat trailer	A Boat trailer is a Trailer (vehicle) designed to launch, retrieve, carry and , boatyards, boat hauliers, boat dealers and boat builders. Generally this type of trailer is not used for storage of the boat.
Employee	Employment is a contract between two parties, one being the employer and the other being the employee. An employee may be defined as: "A person in the service of another under any contract of hire, express or implied, oral or written, where the employer has the power or right to control and direct the employee in the material details of how the work is to be performed." Black"s Law Dictionary page 471 (5th ed. 1979).
	In a commercial setting, the employer conceives of a productive activity, generally with the intention of generating a profit, and the employee contributes labour to the enterprise, usually in return for payment of wages.
Perqs	
	Some of these benefits are: housing (employer-provided or employer-paid), group insurance (health, dental, life etc)., disability income protection, retirement benefits, daycare, tuition reimbursement, sick leave, vacation (paid and non-paid), social security, profit sharing, funding of education, and other specialized benefits.
	The purpose of the benefits is to increase the economic security of employees.
	The term perqs or perks is often used colloquially to refer to those benefits of a more discretionary nature.
IPO	An initial public stock offering (IPO) referred to simply as an "offering" or "flotation," is when a company issues common stock or shares to the public for the first time. They are often issued by smaller, younger companies seeking capital to expand, but can also be done by large privately-owned companies looking to become publicly traded.
	In an IPO the issuer may obtain the assistance of an underwriting firm, which helps it determine what type of security to issue (common or preferred), best offering price and time to bring it to market.
Strategy	A Strategy is a plan of action designed to achieve a particular goal.
	Strategy is different from tactics. In military terms, tactics is concerned with the conduct of an engagement while Strategy is concerned with how different engagements are linked.
Cannibalization	
	Another example of Cannibalization is when a retailer creates a promotion like 20% discount for one item (say Pepsi). The tendency of consumers is to buy the discounted item (Pepsi) rather than the other items with a higher price. However when the promotion event is over, the regular drinker of Coke will resume buying Coke.
Saturation	Saturation or saturated may mean:

· Dew point, which is a temperature that occurs when atmospheric humidity reaches 100% and the air is saturated with moisture

· Market Saturation, in economics, a situation in which a product has become diffused (distributed) within a market

· Saturated model, a concept in mathematical logic

· Saturation (album), an album by the alternative rock band Urge Overkill, created by Overkill corporation, 1994

· Saturation (biology), in mutation studies, the observed number of mutations relative to the maximum amount possible (usually undefined)

· Saturation (chemistry), multiple definitions for chemistry

· Saturation (color theory), the intensity of a specific hue

· Saturation intent, a rendering intent in color management

· Saturation (magnetic), the state when a magnetic material is fully magnetized

· Saturation current, limit of flowing current through a device

· Oxygen Saturation, a clinical measure of the amount of oxygen in a patient"s blood

· Saturation (telecommunications), a number of meanings

· Saturation arithmetic, in arithmetic, a version of arithmetic in which all operations are limited to fixed range

· Saturated fat, fat that consists of triglycerides containing only saturated fatty acid radicals

· In the earth sciences, Saturation generally refers to the water content in the soil, where the unsaturated zone is above the water table and the saturated zone is below

· Saturated liquid or saturated vapor, contains as much thermal energy as it can without boiling or condensing

· Saturated transistor, a BJT transistor or field-effect transistor that is fully turned on "

IPO	An initial public stock offering (IPO) referred to simply as an "offering" or "flotation," is when a company issues common stock or shares to the public for the first time. They are often issued by smaller, younger companies seeking capital to expand, but can also be done by large privately-owned companies looking to become publicly traded.
	In an IPO the issuer may obtain the assistance of an underwriting firm, which helps it determine what type of security to issue (common or preferred), best offering price and time to bring it to market.
SWOT analysis	SWOT analysis is a strategic planning method used to evaluate the Strengths, Weaknesses, Opportunities, and Threats involved in a project or in a business venture. It involves specifying the objective of the business venture or project and identifying the internal and external factors that are favorable and unfavorable to achieving that objective. The technique is credited to Albert Humphrey, who led a research project at Stanford University in the 1960s and 1970s using data from Fortune 500 companies.
Competition	Co-operative competition is based upon promoting mutual survival - "everyone wins". Adam Smith"s "invisible hand" is a process where individuals compete to improve their level of happiness but compete in a cooperative manner through peaceful exchange and without violating other people. Cooperative competition focuses individuals/groups/organisms against the environment.
Standard	A technical standard is an established norm or requirement. It is usually a formal document that establishes uniform engineering or technical criteria, methods, processes and practices.
	A technical standard can also be a controlled artifact or similar formal means used for calibration.
Point	In typography, a point is the smallest unit of measure, being a subdivision of the larger pica. It is commonly abbreviated as pt. The traditional printer"s point, from the era of hot metal typesetting and presswork, varied between 0.18 and 0.4 mm depending on various definitions of the foot.
	Today, the traditional point has been supplanted by the desktop publishing point (also called the PostScript point), which has been rounded to an even 72 points to the inch (1 point = $^{127}/_{360}$ mm $\approx$ 0.353 mm).
Net income	Net income is equal to the income that a firm has after subtracting costs and expenses from the total revenue. Net income can be distributed among holders of common stock as a dividend or held by the firm as retained earnings. Net income is an accounting term.
Trend analysis	The term "Trend analysis" refers to the concept of collecting information and attempting to spot a pattern, in the information. In some fields of study, the term "Trend analysis" has more formally-defined meanings.
	In project management Trend analysis is a mathematical technique that uses historical results to predict future outcome.
Risk	Risk is a concept that denotes the precise probability of specific eventualities. Technically, the notion of Risk is independent from the notion of value and, as such, eventualities may have both beneficial and adverse consequences. However, in general usage the convention is to focus only on potential negative impact to some characteristic of value that may arise from a future event.
Strategy	A Strategy is a plan of action designed to achieve a particular goal.
	Strategy is different from tactics. In military terms, tactics is concerned with the conduct of an engagement while Strategy is concerned with how different engagements are linked.

Initial public stock offering	An initial public stock offering (IPO) referred to simply as an "offering" or "flotation," is when a company issues common stock or shares to the public for the first time. They are often issued by smaller, younger companies seeking capital to expand, but can also be done by large privately-owned companies looking to become publicly traded. In an IPO the issuer may obtain the assistance of an underwriting firm, which helps it determine what type of security to issue (common or preferred), best offering price and time to bring it to market.
Quality	Quality in business, engineering and manufacturing has a pragmatic interpretation as the non-inferiority or superiority of something. Quality is a perceptual, conditional and somewhat subjective attribute and may be understood differently by different people. Consumers may focus on the specification Quality of a product/service, or how it compares to competitors in the marketplace.

Celebrity branding	Celebrity branding is a type of branding, in which a celebrity uses his or her status in society to promote a product, service or charity. Celebrity branding can take several different forms, from a celebrity simply appearing in advertisements for a product, service or charity, to a celebrity attending PR events, creating his or her own line of products or services, and/or using his or her name as a brand. The most popular forms of celebrity brand lines are for clothing and fragrances.
Product	When a product reaches the maturity stage of the product life cycle a company may choose to operate strategies to extend the life of the product. If the product is predicted to continue to be successful or an upgrade is soon to be released the company can use various methods to keep sales, else the product will be left as is to continue to the decline stage.

Examples of extension strategies are:

· Discounted price
· Increased advertising
· Accessing another market abroad

Another strategy is added value.
This is a widely used extension strategy.

Sale	A sale is the pinnacle activity involved in selling products or services in return for money or other compensation. It is an act of completion of a commercial activity.

A sale is completed by the seller, the owner of the goods.

Marketing	

marketing is a "social and managerial process by which individuals and groups obtain what they need and want through creating and exchanging products and values with others." It is an integrated process through which companies create value for customers and build strong customer relationships in order to capture value from customers in return.
marketing is used to create the customer, to keep the customer and to satisfy the customer. With the customer as the focus of its activities, it can be concluded that marketing management is one of the major components of business management.

Marketing research	marketing research is the systematic gathering, recording, and analysis of data about issues relating to marketing products and services. The term is commonly interchanged with market research; however, expert practitioners may wish to draw a distinction, in that market research is concerned specifically with markets, while marketing research is concerned specifically about marketing processes.

marketing research is often partitioned into two sets of categorical pairs, either by target market:

· Consumer marketing research, and
· Business-to-business marketing research

Or, alternatively, by methodological approach:

· Qualitative marketing research, and
· Quantitative marketing research

101

Chapter 5. Cola Wars: Coca-Cola vs. Pepsi

Consumer marketing research is a form of applied sociology that concentrates on understanding the preferences, attitudes, and behaviors of consumers in a market-based economy, and it aims to understand the effects and comparative success of marketing campaigns. The field of consumer marketing research as a statistical science was pioneered by Arthur Nielsen with the founding of the ACNielsen Company in 1923.

Marketing management	Marketing management is a business discipline which is focused on the practical application of marketing techniques and the management of a firm"s marketing resources and activities. Marketing managers are often responsible for influencing the level, timing, and composition of customer demand accepted definition of the term. In part, this is because the role of a marketing manager can vary significantly based on a business" size, corporate culture, and industry context.
Net income	Net income is equal to the income that a firm has after subtracting costs and expenses from the total revenue. Net income can be distributed among holders of common stock as a dividend or held by the firm as retained earnings. Net income is an accounting term.
Need for Achievement	Need for Achievement (N-Ach) refers to an individual"s desire for significant accomplishment, mastering of skills, control, David McClelland.
	Need for Achievement is related to the difficulty of tasks people choose to undertake.

101

Chapter 6. PC Wars: Hewlett-Packard vs. Dell

Data migration	Data migration is the process of transferring data between storage types, formats, freeing up human resources from tedious tasks. It is required when organizations or individuals change computer systems or upgrade to new systems, or when systems merge (such as when the organizations that use them undergo a merger/takeover).
Walt Disney	Walter Elias "Walt" Disney (December 5, 1901 - December 15, 1966) was an American film producer, director, screenwriter, voice actor, animator, entrepreneur, entertainer, international icon and philanthropist. Disney is famous for his influence in the field of entertainment during the twentieth century. As the co-founder (with his brother Roy O. Disney) of Walt Disney Productions, Disney became one of the best-known motion picture producers in the world.
Procter ' Gamble	Procter is a surname, and may also refer to: · Bryan Waller Procter (pseud. Barry Cornwall), English poet · Goodwin Procter, American law firm · Procter ' Gamble, consumer products multinational "
Cash cow	In business, a Cash cow is a product or a business unit that generates unusually high profit margins: so high that it is responsible for a large amount of a company"s operating profit. This profit far exceeds the amount necessary to maintain the Cash cow business, and the excess is used by the business for other purposes. A firm is said to be acting as a Cash cow when its earnings per share (EPS) is equal to its dividends per share (DPS), or in other words, when a firm pays out 100% of its free cash flow (FCF) to its shareholders as dividends at the end of each accounting term.
Customer service	Customer service is the provision of service to customers before, during and after a purchase. According to Jamier L. Scott. (2002), "Customer service is a series of activities designed to enhance the level of customer satisfaction - that is, the feeling that a product or service has met the customer expectation." Its importance varies by product, industry and customer; defective or broken merchandise can be exchanged/swapped, often only with a receipt and within a specified time frame.
Outsourcing	outsourcing is subcontracting a service, such as product design or manufacturing, to a third-party company. The decision whether to outsource or to do inhouse is often based upon achieving a lower production cost, making better use of available resources, focussing energy on the core competencies of a particular business, or just making more efficient use of labor, capital, information technology or land resources. It is essentially a division of labour.
Competition	Co-operative competition is based upon promoting mutual survival - "everyone wins". Adam Smith"s "invisible hand" is a process where individuals compete to improve their level of happiness but compete in a cooperative manner through peaceful exchange and without violating other people. Cooperative competition focuses individuals/groups/organisms against the environment.
Product	When a product reaches the maturity stage of the product life cycle a company may choose to operate strategies to extend the life of the product. If the product is predicted to continue to be successful or an upgrade is soon to be released the company can use various methods to keep sales, else the product will be left as is to continue to the decline stage. Examples of extension strategies are:

· Discounted price
· Increased advertising
· Accessing another market abroad
Another strategy is added value.
This is a widely used extension strategy.

Safety

Safety is the state of being "safe" , the condition of being protected against physical, social, spiritual, financial, political, emotional, occupational, psychological, educational or other types or consequences of failure, damage, error, accidents, harm or any other event which could be considered non-desirable. This can take the form of being protected from the event or from exposure to something that causes health or economical losses. It can include protection of people or of possessions.

Competition	Co-operative competition is based upon promoting mutual survival - "everyone wins". Adam Smith"s "invisible hand" is a process where individuals compete to improve their level of happiness but compete in a cooperative manner through peaceful exchange and without violating other people. Cooperative competition focuses individuals/groups/organisms against the environment.
Market share	Market share, in strategic management and marketing is, according to Carlton O"Neal, the percentage or proportion of the total available market or market segment that is being serviced by a company. It can be expressed as a company"s sales revenue divided by the total sales revenue available in that market. It can also be expressed as a company"s unit sales volume (in a market) divided by the total volume of units sold in that market.
Inventory	Inventory is a list for goods and materials, held available in stock by a business. It is also used for a list of the contents of a household and for a list for testamentary purposes of the possessions of someone who has died. In accounting Inventory is considered an asset.
Southwest Airlines	Southwest Airlines Co. (NYSE: LUV) is an American low-cost airline with its largest focus city at Las Vegas" McCarran International Airport. Southwest is the largest airline in the United States by number of passengers carried domestically per year (as of December 31, 2007.)
Space	space is the boundless, three-dimensional extent in which objects and events occur and have relative position and direction. Physical space is often conceived in three linear dimensions, although modern physicists usually consider it, with time, to be part of the boundless four-dimensional continuum known as space time. In mathematics space s with different numbers of dimensions and with different underlying structures can be examined.
United Airlines	United Air Lines, Inc., trading as United Airlines (NASDAQ: United Airlines United Airlines), is a major airline of the United States. It is a subsidiary of United Airlines L Corporation with corporate offices in Chicago at 77 West Wacker Drive in the Chicago Loop and in the nearby Elk Grove Township. United"s largest hub is O"Hare International Airport, where it has more than 550 daily departures.
Sears	Sears, Roebuck and Co., commonly known as Sears, is an American mid-range chain of international department stores, founded by Richard Warren Sears and Alvah Roebuck in the late 19th century.
	From its mail order beginnings, the company grew to become the largest retailer in the United States by the mid-20th century, and its catalogs became famous. Competition and changes in the demographics of its customer base challenged the company after World War II as its rural and inner city strongholds shrank and the suburban markets grew.
King	The king is a playing card with a picture of a king on it. The usual rank of a king is as if it were a 13; that is, above the queen. In some games, the king is the highest-ranked card; in others, the ace is higher.
Dangerous goods	dangerous goods,), are solids, liquids, other living organisms, property, or the environment. They are often subject to chemical regulations. dangerous goods include materials that are radioactive, flammable, explosive or corrosive, oxidizers or asphyxiants, biohazardous, toxic, pathogen or allergen substances and organisms.

Chapter 7. Airliner Wars: Boeing vs. Airbus; and Recent Outsourcing Woes

Price war

Price war is a term used in business to indicate a state of intense competitive rivalry accompanied by a multi-lateral series of price reduction. One competitor will lower its price, then others will lower their prices to match. If one of them reduces their price again, a new round of reductions starts.

Risk

Risk is a concept that denotes the precise probability of specific eventualities. Technically, the notion of Risk is independent from the notion of value and, as such, eventualities may have both beneficial and adverse consequences. However, in general usage the convention is to focus only on potential negative impact to some characteristic of value that may arise from a future event.

Synergy

Synergy is the term used to describe a situation where different entities cooperate advantageously for a final outcome. Simply defined, it means that the whole is greater than the sum of its parts. The essence of Synergy is to value differences.

Ray Kroc	Ray Kroc took over the (at the time) small-scale McDonald"s Corporation franchise in 1954 and built it into the most successful fast food operation in the world. Kroc was included in Time 100: The Most Important People of the Century, and amassed a $500 million fortune during his lifetime. He was also the owner of the San Diego Padres baseball team starting in 1974.
Consortium	A Consortium is an association of two or more individuals, companies, organizations or governments (or any combination of these entities) with the objective of participating in a common activity or pooling their resources for achieving a common goal. Consortium is a Latin word, meaning "partnership, association or society" and derives from consors "partner", itself from con- "together" and sors "fate", meaning owner of means or comrade. For example, Five Colleges, Inc.
Taco Bell	Taco Bell is a restaurant chain based in Irvine, California, specializing in Mexican-inspired fast food. It is a subsidiary of Yum! Brands. Most restaurants are located in North America, but there are also many in other countries.
Competition	Co-operative competition is based upon promoting mutual survival - "everyone wins". Adam Smith"s "invisible hand" is a process where individuals compete to improve their level of happiness but compete in a cooperative manner through peaceful exchange and without violating other people. Cooperative competition focuses individuals/groups/organisms against the environment.
King	The king is a playing card with a picture of a king on it. The usual rank of a king is as if it were a 13; that is, above the queen. In some games, the king is the highest-ranked card; in others, the ace is higher.
Cannibalization	Another example of Cannibalization is when a retailer creates a promotion like 20% discount for one item (say Pepsi). The tendency of consumers is to buy the discounted item (Pepsi) rather than the other items with a higher price. However when the promotion event is over, the regular drinker of Coke will resume buying Coke.
International business	international business is a term used to collectively describe all commercial transactions (private and governmental, sales, investments, logistics,and transportation) that take place between two or more nations. Usually, private companies undertake such transactions for profit; governments undertake them for profit and for political reasons. A multinational enterprise (MNE) is a company that has a worldwide approach to markets and production or one with operations in more than a country.
Price war	Price war is a term used in business to indicate a state of intense competitive rivalry accompanied by a multi-lateral series of price reduction. One competitor will lower its price, then others will lower their prices to match. If one of them reduces their price again, a new round of reductions starts.
Market share	Market share, in strategic management and marketing is, according to Carlton O"Neal, the percentage or proportion of the total available market or market segment that is being serviced by a company. It can be expressed as a company"s sales revenue divided by the total sales revenue available in that market. It can also be expressed as a company"s unit sales volume (in a market) divided by the total volume of units sold in that market.
Strategy	A Strategy is a plan of action designed to achieve a particular goal.

	Strategy is different from tactics. In military terms, tactics is concerned with the conduct of an engagement while Strategy is concerned with how different engagements are linked.
Pricing	pricing is a fundamental aspect of financial modelling, and is one of the four Ps of the marketing mix. The other three aspects are product, promotion, and place. It is also a key variable in microeconomic price allocation theory.
Standard	A technical standard is an established norm or requirement. It is usually a formal document that establishes uniform engineering or technical criteria, methods, processes and practices.
	A technical standard can also be a controlled artifact or similar formal means used for calibration.

Competition	Co-operative competition is based upon promoting mutual survival - "everyone wins". Adam Smith"s "invisible hand" is a process where individuals compete to improve their level of happiness but compete in a cooperative manner through peaceful exchange and without violating other people. Cooperative competition focuses individuals/groups/organisms against the environment.
IPO	An initial public stock offering (IPO) referred to simply as an "offering" or "flotation," is when a company issues common stock or shares to the public for the first time. They are often issued by smaller, younger companies seeking capital to expand, but can also be done by large privately-owned companies looking to become publicly traded.
	In an IPO the issuer may obtain the assistance of an underwriting firm, which helps it determine what type of security to issue (common or preferred), best offering price and time to bring it to market.
Just-in-time	Just in Time could refer to the following:
	· Just-in-time (business), an inventory strategy that reduces in-process inventory · Just-in-time compilation, a technique for improving the performance of bytecode-compiled programming systems · "Just in Time," a 1956 popular song composed by Jule Styne with lyrics written by Betty Comden and Adolph Green, best known in a recording by Tony Bennett · Just in Time (film), a 2006 British film "
Quality	Quality in business, engineering and manufacturing has a pragmatic interpretation as the non-inferiority or superiority of something. Quality is a perceptual, conditional and somewhat subjective attribute and may be understood differently by different people. Consumers may focus on the specification Quality of a product/service, or how it compares to competitors in the marketplace.
Statistical	Statistics is considered by some to be a mathematical science pertaining to the collection, analysis, interpretation or explanation, and presentation of data, while others consider it to be a branch of mathematics concerned with collecting and interpreting data.Statisticians improve the quality of data with the design of experiments and survey sampling. Statistics also provides tools for prediction and forecasting using data and statistical models. Statistics is applicable to a wide variety of academic disciplines, including natural and social sciences, government, and business.
Inventory	Inventory is a list for goods and materials, held available in stock by a business. It is also used for a list of the contents of a household and for a list for testamentary purposes of the possessions of someone who has died. In accounting Inventory is considered an asset.
Standard	A technical standard is an established norm or requirement. It is usually a formal document that establishes uniform engineering or technical criteria, methods, processes and practices.
	A technical standard can also be a controlled artifact or similar formal means used for calibration.

United Airlines	United Air Lines, Inc., trading as United Airlines (NASDAQ: United Airlines United Airlines), is a major airline of the United States. It is a subsidiary of United Airlines L Corporation with corporate offices in Chicago at 77 West Wacker Drive in the Chicago Loop and in the nearby Elk Grove Township. United"s largest hub is O"Hare International Airport, where it has more than 550 daily departures.
Corporate culture	Organizational culture is an idea in the field of Organizational studies and management which describes the psychology, attitudes, experiences, beliefs and values (personal and cultural values) of an organization. It has been defined as "the specific collection of values and norms that are shared by people and groups in an organization and that control the way they interact with each other and with stakeholders outside the organization." This definition continues to explain organizational values also known as "beliefs and ideas about what kinds of goals members of an organization should pursue and ideas about the appropriate kinds or standards of behavior organizational members should use to achieve these goals. From organizational values develop organizational norms, guidelines or expectations that prescribe appropriate kinds of behavior by employees in particular situations and control the behavior of organizational members towards one another." Organizational culture is not the same as Corporate culture.
Customer satisfaction	Customer satisfaction, a business term, is a measure of how products and services supplied by a company meet or surpass customer expectation. It is seen as a key performance indicator within business and is part of the four perspectives of a Balanced Scorecard. In a competitive marketplace where businesses compete for customers, Customer satisfaction is seen as a key differentiator and increasingly has become a key element of business strategy.
Theory	Although the scientific meaning is by far the more commonly used in academic discourse, it is hardly the only one used, and it would be a mistake to assume from the outset that a given use of the term "theory" in academic literature or discourse is a reference to a scientific or empirically-based theory. Even so, since the use of the term theory in scientific or empirical inquiry is the more common one, it will be discussed first. (Other usages follow in the section labeled "Theories formally and generally.") A theory, in the scientific sense of the word, is an analytic structure designed to explain a set of empirical observations. A scientific theory does two things: · it identifies this set of distinct observations as a class of phenomena, and · makes assertions about the underlying reality that brings about or affects this class. In the scientific or empirical tradition, the term "theory" is reserved for ideas which meet baseline requirements about the kinds of empirical observations made, the methods of classification used, and the consistency of the theory in its application among members of the class to which it pertains.
Clubflyer	A Clubflyer or flyer (also spelled flier or called handbill) is a single page leaflet advertising a nightclub, event, service, community communication.
Southwest Airlines	Southwest Airlines Co. (NYSE: LUV) is an American low-cost airline with its largest focus city at Las Vegas" McCarran International Airport. Southwest is the largest airline in the United States by number of passengers carried domestically per year (as of December 31, 2007.)

Employee	Employment is a contract between two parties, one being the employer and the other being the employee. An employee may be defined as: "A person in the service of another under any contract of hire, express or implied, oral or written, where the employer has the power or right to control and direct the employee in the material details of how the work is to be performed." Black"s Law Dictionary page 471 (5th ed. 1979).
	In a commercial setting, the employer conceives of a productive activity, generally with the intention of generating a profit, and the employee contributes labour to the enterprise, usually in return for payment of wages.
Incentive	In economics and sociology, an Incentive is any factor (financial or non-financial) that enables or motivates a particular course of action, the study of Incentive structures is central to the study of all economic activity (both in terms of individual decision-making and in terms of co-operation and competition within a larger institutional structure).
Competition	Co-operative competition is based upon promoting mutual survival - "everyone wins". Adam Smith"s "invisible hand" is a process where individuals compete to improve their level of happiness but compete in a cooperative manner through peaceful exchange and without violating other people. Cooperative competition focuses individuals/groups/organisms against the environment.
Risk	Risk is a concept that denotes the precise probability of specific eventualities. Technically, the notion of Risk is independent from the notion of value and, as such, eventualities may have both beneficial and adverse consequences. However, in general usage the convention is to focus only on potential negative impact to some characteristic of value that may arise from a future event.

Brand extension	Brand extension or brand stretching is a marketing strategy in which a firm marketing a product with a well-developed image uses the same brand name in a different product category. Organizations use this strategy to increase and leverage brand equity . An example of a Brand extension is Jello-gelatin creating Jello pudding pops.
Lee	Lee is a brand of denim jeans, first produced in 1889 in Salina, Kansas. The company is owned by VF Corporation, the largest apparel company in the world. Its headquarters are currently in Merriam near Kansas City, Kansas.
Strategy	A Strategy is a plan of action designed to achieve a particular goal.
	Strategy is different from tactics. In military terms, tactics is concerned with the conduct of an engagement while Strategy is concerned with how different engagements are linked.
Negative	In statistics, a relationship between two variables is negative if the slope in a corresponding graph is negative, or--what is in some contexts equivalent--if the correlation between them is negative.
	Example: "They observed a negative relationship between illness and vaccination." As incident of vaccination is increasing, incidence of illness is decreasing, and vice versa.
	Compare to a positive relationship: Observed a positive relationship between illness and missed work.
Celebrity branding	Celebrity branding is a type of branding, in which a celebrity uses his or her status in society to promote a product, service or charity. Celebrity branding can take several different forms, from a celebrity simply appearing in advertisements for a product, service or charity, to a celebrity attending PR events, creating his or her own line of products or services, and/or using his or her name as a brand. The most popular forms of celebrity brand lines are for clothing and fragrances.
Product	When a product reaches the maturity stage of the product life cycle a company may choose to operate strategies to extend the life of the product. If the product is predicted to continue to be successful or an upgrade is soon to be released the company can use various methods to keep sales, else the product will be left as is to continue to the decline stage.
	Examples of extension strategies are: · Discounted price · Increased advertising · Accessing another market abroad Another strategy is added value.
	This is a widely used extension strategy.

Lee	Lee is a brand of denim jeans, first produced in 1889 in Salina, Kansas. The company is owned by VF Corporation, the largest apparel company in the world. Its headquarters are currently in Merriam near Kansas City, Kansas.
Standard	A technical standard is an established norm or requirement. It is usually a formal document that establishes uniform engineering or technical criteria, methods, processes and practices.
	A technical standard can also be a controlled artifact or similar formal means used for calibration.

Lee	Lee is a brand of denim jeans, first produced in 1889 in Salina, Kansas. The company is owned by VF Corporation, the largest apparel company in the world. Its headquarters are currently in Merriam near Kansas City, Kansas.
Dangerous goods	dangerous goods,), are solids, liquids, other living organisms, property, or the environment. They are often subject to chemical regulations. dangerous goods include materials that are radioactive, flammable, explosive or corrosive, oxidizers or asphyxiants, biohazardous, toxic, pathogen or allergen substances and organisms.
American Motors	American Motors Corporation (AMC) was an American automobile company formed by the 1954 merger of Nash-Kelvinator Corporation and Hudson Motor Car Company -- at the time, it was the largest corporate merger in U.S. history.
	American Motors (AMC) purchased Kaiser"s Jeep operations in 1970 with Jeep"s utility vehicles complementing AMC"s passenger car business. AMC partnered with France"s Renault, from 1980 to 1987, when Chrysler purchased AMC. Both AMC and Renault brands ceased in the United States, while Jeep and some Eagle models continued under Chrysler.
Volvo	The Volvo Group is a Swedish supplier of commercial vehicles such as trucks, buses and construction equipment, drive systems for marine and industrial applications, aerospace components and financial services. Although Volvo was incorporated in 1915 as a subsidiary of AB SKF, a Swedish ball bearing manufacturer, the auto manufacturer was officially founded on 14 April 1927, when the first car rolled off the factory in Hisingen, Gothenburg.
	Volvo means "I roll" in Latin , conjugated from "volvere" (cp the ball bearing producer SKF.)
Sale	A sale is the pinnacle activity involved in selling products or services in return for money or other compensation. It is an act of completion of a commercial activity.
	A sale is completed by the seller, the owner of the goods.
Rebate	A Rebate is an amount paid by way of reduction, return, or refund on what has already been paid or contributed. It is a type of sales promotion marketers use primarily as incentives or supplements to product sales. The mail-in Rebate is the most common.
Corporate culture	Organizational culture is an idea in the field of Organizational studies and management which describes the psychology, attitudes, experiences, beliefs and values (personal and cultural values) of an organization. It has been defined as "the specific collection of values and norms that are shared by people and groups in an organization and that control the way they interact with each other and with stakeholders outside the organization."
	This definition continues to explain organizational values also known as "beliefs and ideas about what kinds of goals members of an organization should pursue and ideas about the appropriate kinds or standards of behavior organizational members should use to achieve these goals. From organizational values develop organizational norms, guidelines or expectations that prescribe appropriate kinds of behavior by employees in particular situations and control the behavior of organizational members towards one another."
	Organizational culture is not the same as Corporate culture.
Verizon	Verizon Communications Inc. (NYSE: VZ) is an American broadband and telecommunications company and a component of the Dow Jones Industrial Average. It was formed in 2000 when Bell Atlantic, one of the Regional Bell Operating Companies, merged with GTE.

Synergy	Synergy is the term used to describe a situation where different entities cooperate advantageously for a final outcome. Simply defined, it means that the whole is greater than the sum of its parts. The essence of Synergy is to value differences.
Cannibalization	
	Another example of Cannibalization is when a retailer creates a promotion like 20% discount for one item (say Pepsi). The tendency of consumers is to buy the discounted item (Pepsi) rather than the other items with a higher price. However when the promotion event is over, the regular drinker of Coke will resume buying Coke.

Product	When a product reaches the maturity stage of the product life cycle a company may choose to operate strategies to extend the life of the product. If the product is predicted to continue to be successful or an upgrade is soon to be released the company can use various methods to keep sales, else the product will be left as is to continue to the decline stage. Examples of extension strategies are: · Discounted price · Increased advertising · Accessing another market abroad Another strategy is added value. This is a widely used extension strategy.
Power position	power position is a concept from Feng Shui, the ancient Chinese practice of studying one"s position within one"s surroundings. In Feng Shui, the power position or "Dragon Seat" is the physical position in the room for a business meeting, which supposedly has the most power. The person in this position can see all entrances to the room, and they are seated against a wall or other structure, so that no activity occurs behind them.
Negative	In statistics, a relationship between two variables is negative if the slope in a corresponding graph is negative, or--what is in some contexts equivalent--if the correlation between them is negative. Example: "They observed a negative relationship between illness and vaccination." As incident of vaccination is increasing, incidence of illness is decreasing, and vice versa. Compare to a positive relationship: Observed a positive relationship between illness and missed work.
Customer service	Customer service is the provision of service to customers before, during and after a purchase. According to Jamier L. Scott. (2002), "Customer service is a series of activities designed to enhance the level of customer satisfaction - that is, the feeling that a product or service has met the customer expectation." Its importance varies by product, industry and customer; defective or broken merchandise can be exchanged/swapped, often only with a receipt and within a specified time frame.
Competition	Co-operative competition is based upon promoting mutual survival - "everyone wins". Adam Smith"s "invisible hand" is a process where individuals compete to improve their level of happiness but compete in a cooperative manner through peaceful exchange and without violating other people. Cooperative competition focuses individuals/groups/organisms against the environment.
Seasonality	In statistics, many time series exhibit cyclic variation known as seasonality, periodic variation, retail sales tend to peak for the Christmas season and then decline after the holidays.
Restructuring	restructuring is the corporate management term for the act of partially dismantling or otherwise reorganizing a company for the purpose of making it more profitable. Also known as corporate restructuring, debt restructuring and financial restructuring. restructuring is often done as part of a bankruptcy or of a strategic takeover by another firm, such as a leveraged buyout by a private equity firm.

Walt Disney	Walter Elias "Walt" Disney (December 5, 1901 - December 15, 1966) was an American film producer, director, screenwriter, voice actor, animator, entrepreneur, entertainer, international icon and philanthropist. Disney is famous for his influence in the field of entertainment during the twentieth century. As the co-founder (with his brother Roy O. Disney) of Walt Disney Productions, Disney became one of the best-known motion picture producers in the world.
Walt Disney Company	The Walt Disney Company is the largest media and entertainment corporation in the world. Founded on October 16, 1923, by brothers Walt and Roy Disney as an animation studio, it has become one of the biggest Hollywood studios, and owner and licensor of eleven theme parks and several television networks, including ABC and ESPN. Disney"s corporate headquarters and primary production facilities are located at The Walt Disney Studios in Burbank, California.
Pricing	pricing is a fundamental aspect of financial modelling, and is one of the four Ps of the marketing mix. The other three aspects are product, promotion, and place. It is also a key variable in microeconomic price allocation theory.
Point	In typography, a point is the smallest unit of measure, being a subdivision of the larger pica. It is commonly abbreviated as pt. The traditional printer"s point, from the era of hot metal typesetting and presswork, varied between 0.18 and 0.4 mm depending on various definitions of the foot.
	Today, the traditional point has been supplanted by the desktop publishing point (also called the PostScript point), which has been rounded to an even 72 points to the inch (1 point = $127/_{360}$ mm ≈ 0.353 mm).
Marketing	marketing is a "social and managerial process by which individuals and groups obtain what they need and want through creating and exchanging products and values with others." It is an integrated process through which companies create value for customers and build strong customer relationships in order to capture value from customers in return. marketing is used to create the customer, to keep the customer and to satisfy the customer. With the customer as the focus of its activities, it can be concluded that marketing management is one of the major components of business management.
Risk	Risk is a concept that denotes the precise probability of specific eventualities. Technically, the notion of Risk is independent from the notion of value and, as such, eventualities may have both beneficial and adverse consequences. However, in general usage the convention is to focus only on potential negative impact to some characteristic of value that may arise from a future event.

Promotion	Promotion involves disseminating information about a product, product line, brand, or company. It is one of the four key aspects of the marketing mix. (The other three elements are product marketing, pricing, and distribution). P>Promotion is generally sub-divided into two parts:
	· Above the line Promotion: Promotion in the media (e.g. TV, radio, newspapers, Internet and Mobile Phones) in which the advertiser pays an advertising agency to place the ad · Below the line Promotion: All other Promotion. Much of this is intended to be subtle enough for the consumer to be unaware that Promotion is taking place. E.g. sponsorship, product placement, endorsements, sales Promotion, merchandising, direct mail, personal selling, public relations, trade shows
Standard	A technical standard is an established norm or requirement. It is usually a formal document that establishes uniform engineering or technical criteria, methods, processes and practices.
	A technical standard can also be a controlled artifact or similar formal means used for calibration.
Cost-benefit	Cost-benefit analysis is a term that refers both to:
	· helping to appraise, or assess, the case for a project or proposal, which itself is a process known as project appraisal; and · an informal approach to making decisions of any kind. Under both definitions the process involves, whether explicitly or implicitly, weighing the total expected costs against the total expected benefits of one or more actions in order to choose the best or most profitable option. The formal process is often referred to as either CBA (Cost-benefit Analysis) or BCA (Benefit-Cost Analysis).
Cost-benefit analysis	Cost-benefit analysis is a term that refers both to:
	· helping to appraise, or assess, the case for a project or proposal, which itself is a process known as project appraisal; and · an informal approach to making decisions of any kind. Under both definitions the process involves, whether explicitly or implicitly, weighing the total expected costs against the total expected benefits of one or more actions in order to choose the best or most profitable option. The formal process is often referred to as either CBA (Cost-benefit analysis) or BCA (Benefit-Cost Analysis).
Sears	Sears, Roebuck and Co., commonly known as Sears, is an American mid-range chain of international department stores, founded by Richard Warren Sears and Alvah Roebuck in the late 19th century.
	From its mail order beginnings, the company grew to become the largest retailer in the United States by the mid-20th century, and its catalogs became famous. Competition and changes in the demographics of its customer base challenged the company after World War II as its rural and inner city strongholds shrank and the suburban markets grew.
Boat trailer	A Boat trailer is a Trailer (vehicle) designed to launch, retrieve, carry and , boatyards, boat haulers, boat dealers and boat builders. Generally this type of trailer is not used for storage of the boat.

Outsourcing	outsourcing is subcontracting a service, such as product design or manufacturing, to a third-party company. The decision whether to outsource or to do inhouse is often based upon achieving a lower production cost, making better use of available resources, focussing energy on the core competencies of a particular business, or just making more efficient use of labor, capital, information technology or land resources. It is essentially a division of labour.
Corporate culture	Organizational culture is an idea in the field of Organizational studies and management which describes the psychology, attitudes, experiences, beliefs and values (personal and cultural values) of an organization. It has been defined as "the specific collection of values and norms that are shared by people and groups in an organization and that control the way they interact with each other and with stakeholders outside the organization."
	This definition continues to explain organizational values also known as "beliefs and ideas about what kinds of goals members of an organization should pursue and ideas about the appropriate kinds or standards of behavior organizational members should use to achieve these goals. From organizational values develop organizational norms, guidelines or expectations that prescribe appropriate kinds of behavior by employees in particular situations and control the behavior of organizational members towards one another."
	Organizational culture is not the same as Corporate culture.

Chapter 17. Kmart and Sears: A Hedge Fund Manager`s Challenge

Sears	Sears, Roebuck and Co., commonly known as Sears, is an American mid-range chain of international department stores, founded by Richard Warren Sears and Alvah Roebuck in the late 19th century.
	From its mail order beginnings, the company grew to become the largest retailer in the United States by the mid-20th century, and its catalogs became famous. Competition and changes in the demographics of its customer base challenged the company after World War II as its rural and inner city strongholds shrank and the suburban markets grew.
Wal-Mart	Wal-Mart Stores, Inc. is an American public corporation that runs a chain of large, discount department stores. It is the world"s largest public corporation by revenue, according to the 2008 Fortune Global 500.
Sam Walton	Samuel Moore Walton (March 29, 1918 - April 5, 1992) was an American businessman and entrepreneur born in Kingfisher, Oklahoma who founded two American retailers, Wal-Mart and Sam"s Club.
	Sam Walton was born to Thomas Gibson Walton and Nancy "Nannie" Lee Lawrence near Kingfisher, Oklahoma on March 29, 1918. There, he lived with his parents on their farm until 1923.
Competition	Co-operative competition is based upon promoting mutual survival - "everyone wins". Adam Smith"s "invisible hand" is a process where individuals compete to improve their level of happiness but compete in a cooperative manner through peaceful exchange and without violating other people. Cooperative competition focuses individuals/groups/organisms against the environment.
Boat trailer	A Boat trailer is a Trailer (vehicle) designed to launch, retrieve, carry and , boatyards, boat hauliers, boat dealers and boat builders. Generally this type of trailer is not used for storage of the boat.
Synergy	Synergy is the term used to describe a situation where different entities cooperate advantageously for a final outcome. Simply defined, it means that the whole is greater than the sum of its parts. The essence of Synergy is to value differences.

Southwest Airlines	Southwest Airlines Co. (NYSE: LUV) is an American low-cost airline with its largest focus city at Las Vegas" McCarran International Airport. Southwest is the largest airline in the United States by number of passengers carried domestically per year (as of December 31, 2007.)
Bankruptcy	bankruptcy is a legally declared inability or impairment of ability of an individual or organization to pay its creditors. Creditors may file a bankruptcy petition against a debtor ("involuntary bankruptcy") in an effort to recoup a portion of what they are owed or initiate a restructuring. In the majority of cases, however, bankruptcy is initiated by the debtor (a "voluntary bankruptcy" that is filed by the insolvent individual or organization).
SWOT analysis	SWOT analysis is a strategic planning method used to evaluate the Strengths, Weaknesses, Opportunities, and Threats involved in a project or in a business venture. It involves specifying the objective of the business venture or project and identifying the internal and external factors that are favorable and unfavorable to achieving that objective. The technique is credited to Albert Humphrey, who led a research project at Stanford University in the 1960s and 1970s using data from Fortune 500 companies.
Competition	Co-operative competition is based upon promoting mutual survival - "everyone wins". Adam Smith"s "invisible hand" is a process where individuals compete to improve their level of happiness but compete in a cooperative manner through peaceful exchange and without violating other people. Cooperative competition focuses individuals/groups/organisms against the environment.
King	The king is a playing card with a picture of a king on it. The usual rank of a king is as if it were a 13; that is, above the queen. In some games, the king is the highest-ranked card; in others, the ace is higher.
United Airlines	United Air Lines, Inc., trading as United Airlines (NASDAQ: United Airlines United Airlines), is a major airline of the United States. It is a subsidiary of United Airlines L Corporation with corporate offices in Chicago at 77 West Wacker Drive in the Chicago Loop and in the nearby Elk Grove Township. United"s largest hub is O"Hare International Airport, where it has more than 550 daily departures.
Pricing	pricing is a fundamental aspect of financial modelling, and is one of the four Ps of the marketing mix. The other three aspects are product, promotion, and place. It is also a key variable in microeconomic price allocation theory.
Strategy	A Strategy is a plan of action designed to achieve a particular goal.
	Strategy is different from tactics. In military terms, tactics is concerned with the conduct of an engagement while Strategy is concerned with how different engagements are linked.
Customer satisfaction	Customer satisfaction, a business term, is a measure of how products and services supplied by a company meet or surpass customer expectation. It is seen as a key performance indicator within business and is part of the four perspectives of a Balanced Scorecard.
	In a competitive marketplace where businesses compete for customers, Customer satisfaction is seen as a key differentiator and increasingly has become a key element of business strategy.
Employee	Employment is a contract between two parties, one being the employer and the other being the employee. An employee may be defined as: "A person in the service of another under any contract of hire, express or implied, oral or written, where the employer has the power or right to control and direct the employee in the material details of how the work is to be performed." Black"s Law Dictionary page 471 (5th ed. 1979).

57

In a commercial setting, the employer conceives of a productive activity, generally with the intention of generating a profit, and the employee contributes labour to the enterprise, usually in return for payment of wages.

101

Competition	Co-operative competition is based upon promoting mutual survival - "everyone wins". Adam Smith"s "invisible hand" is a process where individuals compete to improve their level of happiness but compete in a cooperative manner through peaceful exchange and without violating other people. Cooperative competition focuses individuals/groups/organisms against the environment.
Reebok	Reebok International Limited, a subsidiary of German sportswear giant Adidas, is a producer of athletic footwear, apparel, and accessories. The name comes from the Afrikaans spelling of rhebok, a type of African antelope or gazelle. The company, founded in Bolton, England in 1895, was originally called J.W. Foster and Sons but was renamed Reebok in 1958.
Shoe	A Shoe is an item of footwear evolved at first to protect the human foot and later, additionally, as an item of decoration in itself. The foot contains more bones than any other single part of the body, and has evolved over hundreds of thousands of years in relation to vastly varied terrain and climatic conditions. Together with the proprioceptive system, it is what makes possible balance and ambulation.
Customer service	Customer service is the provision of service to customers before, during and after a purchase. According to Jamier L. Scott. (2002), "Customer service is a series of activities designed to enhance the level of customer satisfaction - that is, the feeling that a product or service has met the customer expectation." Its importance varies by product, industry and customer; defective or broken merchandise can be exchanged/swapped, often only with a receipt and within a specified time frame.
IPO	An initial public stock offering (IPO) referred to simply as an "offering" or "flotation," is when a company issues common stock or shares to the public for the first time. They are often issued by smaller, younger companies seeking capital to expand, but can also be done by large privately-owned companies looking to become publicly traded. In an IPO the issuer may obtain the assistance of an underwriting firm, which helps it determine what type of security to issue (common or preferred), best offering price and time to bring it to market.
Knight	A Knight was a "gentleman soldier" or member of the warrior class of the Middle Ages in Europe. In other Indo-European languages, cognates of cavalier or rider are more prevalent suggesting a connection to the Knight"s mode of transport. Since antiquity a position of honour and prestige has been held by mounted warriors such as the Greek hippeus and the Roman eques, and Knighthood in the Middle Ages was inextricably linked with horsemanship.
Sears	Sears, Roebuck and Co., commonly known as Sears, is an American mid-range chain of international department stores, founded by Richard Warren Sears and Alvah Roebuck in the late 19th century. From its mail order beginnings, the company grew to become the largest retailer in the United States by the mid-20th century, and its catalogs became famous. Competition and changes in the demographics of its customer base challenged the company after World War II as its rural and inner city strongholds shrank and the suburban markets grew.
Tiger	TIGER Referencing or TIGER/Line is a format used by the United States Census Bureau to describe land attributes such as roads, buildings, rivers, and lakes, as well as areas such as census tracts. TIGER was developed to support and improve the Bureau"s process of taking the Decennial Census. The TIGER files do not contain the census demographic data, but merely the map data.

Restrictive	In semantics, a modifier is said to be restrictive (or defining) if it restricts the reference of its head. For example, in "the red car is fancier than the blue one", red and blue are restrictive, because they restrict which cars car and one are referring to. ("The car is fancier than the one" would make little sense).
Marketing	marketing is a "social and managerial process by which individuals and groups obtain what they need and want through creating and exchanging products and values with others." It is an integrated process through which companies create value for customers and build strong customer relationships in order to capture value from customers in return. marketing is used to create the customer, to keep the customer and to satisfy the customer. With the customer as the focus of its activities, it can be concluded that marketing management is one of the major components of business management.
Marketing Myopia	Marketing myopia is a term used in marketing as well as the title of an important marketing paper written by Theodore Levitt. This paper was first published in 1960 in the Harvard Business Review; a journal of which he was an editor. Some commentators have suggested that its publication marked the beginning of the modern marketing movement.
Mass marketing	Mass marketing is a market coverage strategy in which a firm decides to ignore market segment differences and go after the whole market with one offer. It is type of marketing (or attempting to sell through persuasion) of a product to a wide audience. The idea is to broadcast a message that will reach the largest number of people possible.
Outsourcing	outsourcing is subcontracting a service, such as product design or manufacturing, to a third-party company. The decision whether to outsource or to do inhouse is often based upon achieving a lower production cost, making better use of available resources, focussing energy on the core competencies of a particular business, or just making more efficient use of labor, capital, information technology or land resources. It is essentially a division of labour.
Marketing management	Marketing management is a business discipline which is focused on the practical application of marketing techniques and the management of a firm"s marketing resources and activities. Marketing managers are often responsible for influencing the level, timing, and composition of customer demand accepted definition of the term. In part, this is because the role of a marketing manager can vary significantly based on a business" size, corporate culture, and industry context.
Role	A role or a social role is a set of connected behaviors, rights and obligations as conceptualized by actors in a social situation. It is an expected behavior in a given individual social status and social position. It is vital to both functionalist and interactionist understandings of society.
Ray Kroc	Ray Kroc took over the (at the time) small-scale McDonald"s Corporation franchise in 1954 and built it into the most successful fast food operation in the world. Kroc was included in Time 100: The Most Important People of the Century, and amassed a $500 million fortune during his lifetime. He was also the owner of the San Diego Padres baseball team starting in 1974.
Lee	Lee is a brand of denim jeans, first produced in 1889 in Salina, Kansas. The company is owned by VF Corporation, the largest apparel company in the world. Its headquarters are currently in Merriam near Kansas City, Kansas.

| Sam Walton | Samuel Moore Walton (March 29, 1918 - April 5, 1992) was an American businessman and entrepreneur born in Kingfisher, Oklahoma who founded two American retailers, Wal-Mart and Sam"s Club. |
| | Sam Walton was born to Thomas Gibson Walton and Nancy "Nannie" Lee Lawrence near Kingfisher, Oklahoma on March 29, 1918. There, he lived with his parents on their farm until 1923. |

Competition	Co-operative competition is based upon promoting mutual survival - "everyone wins". Adam Smith"s "invisible hand" is a process where individuals compete to improve their level of happiness but compete in a cooperative manner through peaceful exchange and without violating other people. Cooperative competition focuses individuals/groups/organisms against the environment.
Index fund	An Index fund or index tracker is a collective investment scheme (usually a mutual fund or exchange-traded fund) that aims to replicate the movements of an index of a specific financial market, regardless of market conditions. Tracking can be achieved by trying to hold all of the securities in the index, in the same proportions as the index. Other methods include statistically sampling the market and holding "representative" securities.
Publicity	publicity is the deliberate attempt to manage the public"s perception of a subject. The subjects of publicity include people (for example, politicians and performing artists), goods and services, organizations of all kinds, and works of art or entertainment. From a marketing perspective, publicity is one component of promotion.
Celebrity branding	Celebrity branding is a type of branding, in which a celebrity uses his or her status in society to promote a product, service or charity. Celebrity branding can take several different forms, from a celebrity simply appearing in advertisements for a product, service or charity, to a celebrity attending PR events, creating his or her own line of products or services, and/or using his or her name as a brand. The most popular forms of celebrity brand lines are for clothing and fragrances.
Product	When a product reaches the maturity stage of the product life cycle a company may choose to operate strategies to extend the life of the product. If the product is predicted to continue to be successful or an upgrade is soon to be released the company can use various methods to keep sales, else the product will be left as is to continue to the decline stage. Examples of extension strategies are: · Discounted price · Increased advertising · Accessing another market abroad Another strategy is added value. This is a widely used extension strategy.
Marketing	marketing is a "social and managerial process by which individuals and groups obtain what they need and want through creating and exchanging products and values with others." It is an integrated process through which companies create value for customers and build strong customer relationships in order to capture value from customers in return. marketing is used to create the customer, to keep the customer and to satisfy the customer. With the customer as the focus of its activities, it can be concluded that marketing management is one of the major components of business management.
Strategy	A Strategy is a plan of action designed to achieve a particular goal.

Strategy is different from tactics. In military terms, tactics is concerned with the conduct of an engagement while Strategy is concerned with how different engagements are linked.

Rofecoxib	Rofecoxib is a nonsteroidal anti-inflammatory drug that has now been withdrawn over safety concerns. It was marketed by Merck ' Co. to treat osteoarthritis, acute pain conditions, and dysmenorrhoea.
Celebrity branding	Celebrity branding is a type of branding, in which a celebrity uses his or her status in society to promote a product, service or charity. Celebrity branding can take several different forms, from a celebrity simply appearing in advertisements for a product, service or charity, to a celebrity attending PR events, creating his or her own line of products or services, and/or using his or her name as a brand. The most popular forms of celebrity brand lines are for clothing and fragrances.
Marketing	marketing is a "social and managerial process by which individuals and groups obtain what they need and want through creating and exchanging products and values with others." It is an integrated process through which companies create value for customers and build strong customer relationships in order to capture value from customers in return. marketing is used to create the customer, to keep the customer and to satisfy the customer. With the customer as the focus of its activities, it can be concluded that marketing management is one of the major components of business management.
Product	When a product reaches the maturity stage of the product life cycle a company may choose to operate strategies to extend the life of the product. If the product is predicted to continue to be successful or an upgrade is soon to be released the company can use various methods to keep sales, else the product will be left as is to continue to the decline stage. Examples of extension strategies are: · Discounted price · Increased advertising · Accessing another market abroad Another strategy is added value. This is a widely used extension strategy.
Relative risk	In statistics and mathematical epidemiology, Relative risk is the risk of an event (or of developing a disease) relative to exposure. Relative risk is a ratio of the probability of the event occurring in the exposed group versus a non-exposed group. $$RR = \frac{p_{\text{exposed}}}{p_{\text{non-exposed}}}$$ Consider an example where the probability of developing lung cancer among smokers was 20% and among non-smokers 1%.
Risk	Risk is a concept that denotes the precise probability of specific eventualities. Technically, the notion of Risk is independent from the notion of value and, as such, eventualities may have both beneficial and adverse consequences. However, in general usage the convention is to focus only on potential negative impact to some characteristic of value that may arise from a future event.
Strategy	A Strategy is a plan of action designed to achieve a particular goal.

Strategy is different from tactics. In military terms, tactics is concerned with the conduct of an engagement while Strategy is concerned with how different engagements are linked.

Corporate culture

Organizational culture is an idea in the field of Organizational studies and management which describes the psychology, attitudes, experiences, beliefs and values (personal and cultural values) of an organization. It has been defined as "the specific collection of values and norms that are shared by people and groups in an organization and that control the way they interact with each other and with stakeholders outside the organization."

This definition continues to explain organizational values also known as "beliefs and ideas about what kinds of goals members of an organization should pursue and ideas about the appropriate kinds or standards of behavior organizational members should use to achieve these goals. From organizational values develop organizational norms, guidelines or expectations that prescribe appropriate kinds of behavior by employees in particular situations and control the behavior of organizational members towards one another."

Organizational culture is not the same as Corporate culture.

Celebrity branding	Celebrity branding is a type of branding, in which a celebrity uses his or her status in society to promote a product, service or charity. Celebrity branding can take several different forms, from a celebrity simply appearing in advertisements for a product, service or charity, to a celebrity attending PR events, creating his or her own line of products or services, and/or using his or her name as a brand. The most popular forms of celebrity brand lines are for clothing and fragrances.
Standard	A technical standard is an established norm or requirement. It is usually a formal document that establishes uniform engineering or technical criteria, methods, processes and practices.
	A technical standard can also be a controlled artifact or similar formal means used for calibration.
Product	When a product reaches the maturity stage of the product life cycle a company may choose to operate strategies to extend the life of the product. If the product is predicted to continue to be successful or an upgrade is soon to be released the company can use various methods to keep sales, else the product will be left as is to continue to the decline stage.
	Examples of extension strategies are:
	· Discounted price · Increased advertising · Accessing another market abroad Another strategy is added value. This is a widely used extension strategy.
Incentive	In economics and sociology, an Incentive is any factor (financial or non-financial) that enables or motivates a particular course of action, the study of Incentive structures is central to the study of all economic activity (both in terms of individual decision-making and in terms of co-operation and competition within a larger institutional structure).

Safety	Safety is the state of being "safe" , the condition of being protected against physical, social, spiritual, financial, political, emotional, occupational, psychological, educational or other types or consequences of failure, damage, error, accidents, harm or any other event which could be considered non-desirable. This can take the form of being protected from the event or from exposure to something that causes health or economical losses. It can include protection of people or of possessions.
Volvo	The Volvo Group is a Swedish supplier of commercial vehicles such as trucks, buses and construction equipment, drive systems for marine and industrial applications, aerospace components and financial services. Although Volvo was incorporated in 1915 as a subsidiary of AB SKF, a Swedish ball bearing manufacturer, the auto manufacturer was officially founded on 14 April 1927, when the first car rolled off the factory in Hisingen, Gothenburg.
	Volvo means "I roll" in Latin , conjugated from "volvere" (cp the ball bearing producer SKF.)
Competition	Co-operative competition is based upon promoting mutual survival - "everyone wins". Adam Smith"s "invisible hand" is a process where individuals compete to improve their level of happiness but compete in a cooperative manner through peaceful exchange and without violating other people. Cooperative competition focuses individuals/groups/organisms against the environment.
Standard	A technical standard is an established norm or requirement. It is usually a formal document that establishes uniform engineering or technical criteria, methods, processes and practices.
	A technical standard can also be a controlled artifact or similar formal means used for calibration.
Product	When a product reaches the maturity stage of the product life cycle a company may choose to operate strategies to extend the life of the product. If the product is predicted to continue to be successful or an upgrade is soon to be released the company can use various methods to keep sales, else the product will be left as is to continue to the decline stage.
	Examples of extension strategies are:
	· Discounted price · Increased advertising · Accessing another market abroad Another strategy is added value. This is a widely used extension strategy.
National Traffic and Motor Vehicle Safety Act	National Traffic and Motor Vehicle Safety Act allowed new standards to be set by the federal government. Regulation of these standards is also managed by the federal government.
	The reduction of the rate of death attributable to motor-vehicle crashes in the United States represents the successful public health response to a great technologic advance of the 20th century--the motorization of America. Six times as many people drive today as in 1925, and the number of motor vehicles in the country has increased 11-fold since then to approximately 215 million The distance traveled in motor vehicles is 10 times higher than in the mid-1920s.
Vehicle	A Vehicle is a mechanical means of conveyance, a carriage or transport. Most often they are manufactured , although some other means of transport which are not made by humans also may be called Vehicles; examples include icebergs and floating tree trunks.

Vehicles may be propelled or pulled by engines or animals including humans, for instance, a chariot, a stagecoach, a mule-drawn barge, an ox-cart or rickshaw.

Groupthink

Groupthink is a type of thought exhibited by group members who try to minimize conflict and reach consensus without critically testing, analyzing, and evaluating ideas. Individual creativity, uniqueness, and independent thinking are lost in the pursuit of group cohesiveness, as are the advantages of reasonable balance in choice and thought that might normally be obtained by making decisions as a group. During Groupthink, members of the group avoid promoting viewpoints outside the comfort zone of consensus thinking.

Strategy

A Strategy is a plan of action designed to achieve a particular goal.

Strategy is different from tactics. In military terms, tactics is concerned with the conduct of an engagement while Strategy is concerned with how different engagements are linked.

Marketing	marketing is a "social and managerial process by which individuals and groups obtain what they need and want through creating and exchanging products and values with others." It is an integrated process through which companies create value for customers and build strong customer relationships in order to capture value from customers in return. marketing is used to create the customer, to keep the customer and to satisfy the customer. With the customer as the focus of its activities, it can be concluded that marketing management is one of the major components of business management.
Marketing management	Marketing management is a business discipline which is focused on the practical application of marketing techniques and the management of a firm"s marketing resources and activities. Marketing managers are often responsible for influencing the level, timing, and composition of customer demand accepted definition of the term. In part, this is because the role of a marketing manager can vary significantly based on a business" size, corporate culture, and industry context.
Southwest Airlines	Southwest Airlines Co. (NYSE: LUV) is an American low-cost airline with its largest focus city at Las Vegas" McCarran International Airport. Southwest is the largest airline in the United States by number of passengers carried domestically per year (as of December 31, 2007.)
Walt Disney	Walter Elias "Walt" Disney (December 5, 1901 - December 15, 1966) was an American film producer, director, screenwriter, voice actor, animator, entrepreneur, entertainer, international icon and philanthropist. Disney is famous for his influence in the field of entertainment during the twentieth century. As the co-founder (with his brother Roy O. Disney) of Walt Disney Productions, Disney became one of the best-known motion picture producers in the world.
Walt Disney Company	The Walt Disney Company is the largest media and entertainment corporation in the world. Founded on October 16, 1923, by brothers Walt and Roy Disney as an animation studio, it has become one of the biggest Hollywood studios, and owner and licensor of eleven theme parks and several television networks, including ABC and ESPN. Disney"s corporate headquarters and primary production facilities are located at The Walt Disney Studios in Burbank, California.
Competition	Co-operative competition is based upon promoting mutual survival - "everyone wins". Adam Smith"s "invisible hand" is a process where individuals compete to improve their level of happiness but compete in a cooperative manner through peaceful exchange and without violating other people. Cooperative competition focuses individuals/groups/organisms against the environment.
King	The king is a playing card with a picture of a king on it. The usual rank of a king is as if it were a 13; that is, above the queen. In some games, the king is the highest-ranked card; in others, the ace is higher.
Dangerous goods	dangerous goods,), are solids, liquids, other living organisms, property, or the environment. They are often subject to chemical regulations. dangerous goods include materials that are radioactive, flammable, explosive or corrosive, oxidizers or asphyxiants, biohazardous, toxic, pathogen or allergen substances and organisms.
Restrictive	In semantics, a modifier is said to be restrictive (or defining) if it restricts the reference of its head. For example, in "the red car is fancier than the blue one", red and blue are restrictive, because they restrict which cars car and one are referring to. ("The car is fancier than the one" would make little sense).

Activism	Activism, in a general sense, can be described as intentional action to bring about social change, political change, economic justice, or opposition to, one side of an often controversial argument.
	The word "Activism" is often used synonymously with protest or dissent, but Activism can stem from any number of political orientations and take a wide range of forms, from writing letters to newspapers or politicians, political campaigning, economic Activism (such as boycotts or preferentially patronizing preferred businesses), rallies, street marches, strikes, both work stoppages and hunger strikes, or even guerrilla tactics.
La Clandestine Absinthe	La Clandestine Absinthe is a Swiss La Bleue, absinthe brand produced by Artemisia-Bugnon distilleries. It is an anise-flavored, distilled liquor containing the herb wormwood (Artemisia absinthium), and when prepared with cold water will louche.
	La Clandestine Absinthe comes in four main styles, as detailed below.
Saturation	Saturation or saturated may mean:
	· Dew point, which is a temperature that occurs when atmospheric humidity reaches 100% and the air is saturated with moisture
	· Market Saturation, in economics, a situation in which a product has become diffused (distributed) within a market
	· Saturated model, a concept in mathematical logic
	· Saturation (album), an album by the alternative rock band Urge Overkill, created by Overkill corporation, 1994
	· Saturation (biology), in mutation studies, the observed number of mutations relative to the maximum amount possible (usually undefined)
	· Saturation (chemistry), multiple definitions for chemistry
	· Saturation (color theory), the intensity of a specific hue
	· Saturation intent, a rendering intent in color management
	· Saturation (magnetic), the state when a magnetic material is fully magnetized
	· Saturation current, limit of flowing current through a device
	· Oxygen Saturation, a clinical measure of the amount of oxygen in a patient"s blood
	· Saturation (telecommunications), a number of meanings
	· Saturation arithmetic, in arithmetic, a version of arithmetic in which all operations are limited to fixed range
	· Saturated fat, fat that consists of triglycerides containing only saturated fatty acid radicals
	· In the earth sciences, Saturation generally refers to the water content in the soil, where the unsaturated zone is above the water table and the saturated zone is below
	· Saturated liquid or saturated vapor, contains as much thermal energy as it can without boiling or condensing
	· Saturated transistor, a BJT transistor or field-effect transistor that is fully turned on "
Product	When a product reaches the maturity stage of the product life cycle a company may choose to operate strategies to extend the life of the product. If the product is predicted to continue to be successful or an upgrade is soon to be released the company can use various methods to keep sales, else the product will be left as is to continue to the decline stage.
	Examples of extension strategies are:
	· Discounted price
	· Increased advertising
	· Accessing another market abroad

Another strategy is added value.

This is a widely used extension strategy.

Merger mania	The term "merger mania" is used, as in financial and law journals, to describe a period of high activity in corporate mergers and acquisitions (M'A), with some merged companies then merging yet again into other companies within a few years. The term has been used for more than 37 years.
	The term merger mania is often used to describe the business activities of the 1990s, where many companies (or corporations), formerly separate for decades, were frequently merged, then some re-merged into other companies, within a few years, with the resulting merged companies sometimes declaring bankruptcy.
Safety	Safety is the state of being "safe" , the condition of being protected against physical, social, spiritual, financial, political, emotional, occupational, psychological, educational or other types or consequences of failure, damage, error, accidents, harm or any other event which could be considered non-desirable. This can take the form of being protected from the event or from exposure to something that causes health or economical losses. It can include protection of people or of possessions.
Environmental monitoring	Environmental monitoring describes the processes and activities that need to take place to characterise and monitor the quality of the environment. Environmental monitoring is used in the preparation of environmental impact assessments, as well as in many circumstances in which human activities carry a risk of harmful effects on the natural environment. All monitoring strategies and programmes have reasons and justifications which are often designed to establish the current status of an environment or to establish trends in environmental parameters.
Risk	Risk is a concept that denotes the precise probability of specific eventualities. Technically, the notion of Risk is independent from the notion of value and, as such, eventualities may have both beneficial and adverse consequences. However, in general usage the convention is to focus only on potential negative impact to some characteristic of value that may arise from a future event.
Point	In typography, a point is the smallest unit of measure, being a subdivision of the larger pica. It is commonly abbreviated as pt. The traditional printer"s point, from the era of hot metal typesetting and presswork, varied between 0.18 and 0.4 mm depending on various definitions of the foot.
	Today, the traditional point has been supplanted by the desktop publishing point (also called the PostScript point), which has been rounded to an even 72 points to the inch (1 point = $127/_{360}$ mm ≈ 0.353 mm).
Vulnerability	For other uses of the word "Vulnerability", please refer to Vulnerability (computing) You may also want to refer to natural disaster.
	Vulnerability is the susceptibility to physical or emotional injury or attack. It also means to have one"s guard down, open to censure or criticism.
Strategy	A Strategy is a plan of action designed to achieve a particular goal.
	Strategy is different from tactics. In military terms, tactics is concerned with the conduct of an engagement while Strategy is concerned with how different engagements are linked.

Celebrity branding	Celebrity branding is a type of branding, in which a celebrity uses his or her status in society to promote a product, service or charity. Celebrity branding can take several different forms, from a celebrity simply appearing in advertisements for a product, service or charity, to a celebrity attending PR events, creating his or her own line of products or services, and/or using his or her name as a brand. The most popular forms of celebrity brand lines are for clothing and fragrances.
Standard	A technical standard is an established norm or requirement. It is usually a formal document that establishes uniform engineering or technical criteria, methods, processes and practices. A technical standard can also be a controlled artifact or similar formal means used for calibration.
Feedback	When Feedback modifies an event/phenomenon, the modification will subsequently influence the Feedback signal in one of three ways: · 1 - the Feedback signal increases, leading to more modification. This is known as positive Feedback. · 2 - the Feedback signal decreases, leading to less modification. This is known as negative Feedback. · 3 - the Feedback signal does not change, indicating the phenomenon is in equilibrium. · Note that an increase or decrease of the Feedback signal here refers to the magnitude of the signal"s absolute value, without regard to the polarity or sign of the signal.
Marketing research	marketing research is the systematic gathering, recording, and analysis of data about issues relating to marketing products and services. The term is commonly interchanged with market research; however, expert practitioners may wish to draw a distinction, in that market research is concerned specifically with markets, while marketing research is concerned specifically about marketing processes. marketing research is often partitioned into two sets of categorical pairs, either by target market: · Consumer marketing research, and · Business-to-business marketing research Or, alternatively, by methodological approach: · Qualitative marketing research, and · Quantitative marketing research Consumer marketing research is a form of applied sociology that concentrates on understanding the preferences, attitudes, and behaviors of consumers in a market-based economy, and it aims to understand the effects and comparative success of marketing campaigns. The field of consumer marketing research as a statistical science was pioneered by Arthur Nielsen with the founding of the ACNielsen Company in 1923.
Targeted advertising	Targeted advertising is a type of advertising whereby advertisements are placed so as to reach consumers based on various traits such as demographics, purchase history, or observed behavior. Two principal forms of targeted interactive advertising are behavioral targeting and contextual advertising.
Offensive	An offensive is a military operation that seeks through aggressive projection of armed force to occupy territory, gain an objective or achieve some larger strategic, operational or tactical goal. Another term for an offensive often used by the media is "invasion", or the more general "attack".

| | The offensive was considered a pre-eminent means of producing victory, although with the recognition of a defensive phase at some stage of the execution. |

| Cost-benefit | Cost-benefit analysis is a term that refers both to: |

· helping to appraise, or assess, the case for a project or proposal, which itself is a process known as project appraisal; and
· an informal approach to making decisions of any kind.
Under both definitions the process involves, whether explicitly or implicitly, weighing the total expected costs against the total expected benefits of one or more actions in order to choose the best or most profitable option. The formal process is often referred to as either CBA (Cost-benefit Analysis) or BCA (Benefit-Cost Analysis).

| Cost-benefit analysis | Cost-benefit analysis is a term that refers both to: |

· helping to appraise, or assess, the case for a project or proposal, which itself is a process known as project appraisal; and
· an informal approach to making decisions of any kind.
Under both definitions the process involves, whether explicitly or implicitly, weighing the total expected costs against the total expected benefits of one or more actions in order to choose the best or most profitable option. The formal process is often referred to as either CBA (Cost-benefit analysis) or BCA (Benefit-Cost Analysis).

| SWOT analysis | SWOT analysis is a strategic planning method used to evaluate the Strengths, Weaknesses, Opportunities, and Threats involved in a project or in a business venture. It involves specifying the objective of the business venture or project and identifying the internal and external factors that are favorable and unfavorable to achieving that objective. The technique is credited to Albert Humphrey, who led a research project at Stanford University in the 1960s and 1970s using data from Fortune 500 companies. |

| Quality | Quality in business, engineering and manufacturing has a pragmatic interpretation as the non-inferiority or superiority of something. Quality is a perceptual, conditional and somewhat subjective attribute and may be understood differently by different people. Consumers may focus on the specification Quality of a product/service, or how it compares to competitors in the marketplace. |

| Employee | Employment is a contract between two parties, one being the employer and the other being the employee. An employee may be defined as: "A person in the service of another under any contract of hire, express or implied, oral or written, where the employer has the power or right to control and direct the employee in the material details of how the work is to be performed." Black"s Law Dictionary page 471 (5th ed. 1979). |

In a commercial setting, the employer conceives of a productive activity, generally with the intention of generating a profit, and the employee contributes labour to the enterprise, usually in return for payment of wages.

| Outsourcing | outsourcing is subcontracting a service, such as product design or manufacturing, to a third-party company. The decision whether to outsource or to do inhouse is often based upon achieving a lower production cost, making better use of available resources, focussing energy on the core competencies of a particular business, or just making more efficient use of labor, capital, information technology or land resources. It is essentially a division of labour. |

Consideration	Consideration is the legal concept of value in connection with contracts. It is anything of value in the common sense, promised to another when making a contract. It can take the form of money, physical objects, services, promised actions, or even abstinence from a future action.
Entrepreneurship	For Frank H. Knight (1921) and Peter Drucker (1970) entrepreneurship is about taking risk. The behavior of the entrepreneur reflects a kind of person willing to put his or her career and financial security on the line and take risks in the name of an idea, spending much time as well as capital on an uncertain venture. Knight classified three types of uncertainty. · Risk, which is measurable statistically . · Ambiguity, which is hard to measure statistically . · True Uncertainty or Knightian Uncertainty, which is impossible to estimate or predict statistically .